New Jersey

Facts and Symbols

by
Shelley Swanson Sateren

Consultant:
Amy Buelow, Teacher
Allendale, New Jersey, School District
New Jersey Council for the Social Studies

Hilltop Books

an imprint of Capstone Press
Mankato, Minnesota

Hilltop Books are published by Capstone Press
818 North Willow Street, Mankato, Minnesota 56001
http://www.capstone-press.com

Library of Congress Cataloging-in-Publication Data
Sateren, Shelley Swanson.
    New Jersey facts and symbols/by Shelley Swanson Sateren.
    p. cm.—(The states and their symbols)
    Includes bibliographical references and index.
    Summary: Presents information about the state of New Jersey, its nickname, flag, motto,
and emblems.
    ISBN 0-7368-0379-3
    1. Emblems, State—New Jersey—Juvenile literature. [1. Emblems, State—New Jersey.
2. New Jersey.] I. Title. II. Series.
CR203.N68S27 2000
974.9—dc21   99-31783
                                                                                                        CIP

Editorial Credits
Christy Steele, editor; Heather Kindseth, cover designer; Linda Clavel, illustrator; Kimberly
    Danger, photo researcher

Photo Credits
Bruce Coleman Inc./Erwin and Peggy Bauer, 6
One Mile Up, Inc., 8, 10 (inset)
Photo Network/Robert K. Grubbs, 12; Jeff Greenberg, 22 (top)
Photophile/Roger Holden, 18; Mark Gibson, 22 (bottom)
Robert McCaw, cover
Root Resources/Pat Wadecki, 16
Unicorn Stock Photos/Andre Jenny, 10; Phyllis Kedl, 14; Joe Sohm, 22 (middle)
Visuals Unlimited/Gary Meszaros, 20

Table of Contents

New York

Connecticut

New York

Edison National
Historic Site 🏛

Newark ●

Pennsylvania

Delaware River

⭐ Trenton

🏛 New Jersey
State Aquarium

Haddonfield ●

**NEW
JERSEY**

Maryland

Delaware

Atlantic Ocean

Atlantic City
Boardwalk 🏛

○	City
⭐	Capital
〰	River
🏛	Places to Visit

Fast Facts

Capital: Trenton is New Jersey's capital.

Largest City: Newark is New Jersey's largest city. About 268,510 people live in Newark.

Size: New Jersey covers 8,215 square miles (21,277 square kilometers). It is the 46th largest state.

Location: New Jersey is in the eastern United States. It is a Mid-Atlantic state.

Population: 8,115,011 people live in New Jersey (U.S. Census Bureau, 1998 estimate).

Statehood: New Jersey became the third state to join the United States on December 18, 1787.

Natural Resources: New Jersey has crushed stone, sand, and gravel. The state also has pine lumber.

Manufactured Goods: Workers in New Jersey make medicines, electronic equipment, chemicals, and food products.

Crops: New Jersey farmers grow tomatoes, blueberries, spinach, cranberries, and peaches. Farmers also raise cattle, sheep, and pigs.

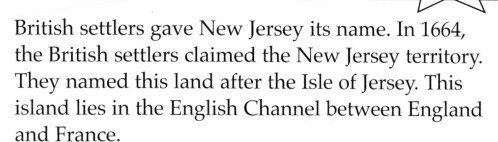

State Name and Nickname

British settlers gave New Jersey its name. In 1664, the British settlers claimed the New Jersey territory. They named this land after the Isle of Jersey. This island lies in the English Channel between England and France.

New Jersey's best-known nickname is the Garden State. Rural New Jersey has many farms. Farmers grow flowers, fruits, and vegetables. New Jersey is the United States' second-largest producer of peaches, spinach, and blueberries. The state is third in the production of cranberries and bell peppers. New Jerseyans also grow cucumbers, lettuce, and asparagus.

Another nickname for New Jersey is the Clam State. Many New Jerseyans dig for clams along the shore of the Atlantic Ocean. New Jersey has about 1,790 miles (2,880 kilometers) of shoreline.

Many New Jerseyans dig for clams on sandbars. These long, narrow masses of sand form near ocean shores.

State Seal and Motto

New Jersey adopted its state seal in 1776. The seal reminds New Jerseyans of their state's government. The seal also makes government papers official.

New Jersey's state seal shows two goddesses, Liberty and Ceres. Liberty represents freedom. Ceres stands for agriculture. Ceres holds a cornucopia full of fruit. Cornucopias also are called horns of plenty. The cornucopia stands for the large amount of crops produced in New Jersey.

Three plows appear on a shield in the center of the seal. The plows stand for the importance of farming to New Jersey. A helmet lies above the shield. The helmet faces forward to suggest that New Jerseyans value leadership and excellence.

New Jersey's state motto is "Liberty and Prosperity." New Jerseyans believe in working hard for freedom and good fortune.

The year 1776 at the bottom of the state seal stands for the year New Jersey declared its independence from England.

State Capitol and Flag

New Jersey's capitol building is in Trenton. Trenton is the capital of New Jersey. Government officials meet in the capitol to make the state's laws.

Workers built New Jersey's capitol in 1792. This building is the second oldest capitol in the United States. Fire destroyed much of the capitol in 1885. Workers finished repairing the building in 1889. Since then, workers have built additions to add space for more offices.

The Senate Chamber is a room in the capitol where state senators meet. Sixteen large paintings called murals decorate the chamber. Each mural shows an important part of New Jersey's history or economy.

The New Jersey government adopted the state flag in 1896. The flag is a light tan color called buff. The state seal is in the center of the flag.

New Jersey's flag is based on its Revolutionary War (1775–1783) battle flag. General George Washington ordered the battle flag's color to be buff in 1779.

State Bird

State officials named the eastern goldfinch New Jersey's state bird in 1935. Many eastern goldfinches live in New Jersey.

The eastern goldfinch has markings that are easy to recognize. Females are dull yellow. Males are bright yellow during spring. In winter, males turn dull yellow like females. Both male and female eastern goldfinches have black wings with white edges. Males also have black foreheads.

Eastern goldfinches build nests in July or August. They use grass and bark to build their nests in bushes. In late summer, females lay four to six pale blue eggs in the nests. The eggs hatch two weeks later.

Females feed seeds to newly hatched young. Eastern goldfinches eat sunflower seeds, hemp seeds, lettuce, and thistles. Young goldfinches fly with their parents until they can care for themselves.

Some people call the eastern goldfinch the American goldfinch or the wild canary.

State Tree

Officials named the red oak New Jersey's state tree in 1950. Red oaks are native to New Jersey. These trees grow in New Jersey's forests. New Jerseyans plant red oaks along many streets.

Red oaks are large trees. They grow 60 to 80 feet (18 to 24 meters) tall. Their trunks grow 2 to 4 feet (61 to 122 centimeters) wide. Dark brown bark with wide, deep cracks covers the trunks.

Red oaks have green leaves with many sharp ends called lobes. These leaves grow 5 to 8 inches (13 to 20 centimeters) long. In autumn, the leaves turn red and fall to the ground. Red oaks grow new leaves each spring.

Red oak trees grow oval-shaped acorns. Oak seeds grow inside these nuts. Acorns can grow up to 1 inch (2.5 centimeters) long. Squirrels and other animals eat the acorns.

Red oaks were named for the red color of their leaves in autumn.

New Jersey garden club members wanted the purple violet to be the state flower. The members' choice became official in 1971.

More than 100 kinds of violets grow in North America. Most violets grow in the eastern United States. New Jersey's woodlands are full of purple violets. The wildflowers also are known as common meadow violets or wooly blue violets.

Purple violets grow close to the ground. They have fuzzy stalks and leafy stems. The green, heart-shaped leaves are 2 to 4 inches (5 to 10 centimeters) long.

Purple violets bloom in spring. Each blossom is about 1 inch (2.5 centimeters) wide. Five purple petals surround the blossom's yellow center.

Some New Jerseyans call the purple violet the Jersey Gem.

State Animal

Two New Jersey students thought the horse should be New Jersey's state animal. The governor made the students' choice the state animal in 1977. A horse's head is on New Jersey's state seal. The horse is a symbol of strength to New Jerseyans.

Horses are an important part of New Jersey's economy. New Jersey has about 7,100 horse farms. On these farms, farmers raise horses to sell. New Jerseyans own more than 600,000 horses. Horse racing is a popular New Jersey sport.

The U.S. Equestrian Team trains in New Jersey. Members of this team compete in horse shows for prizes. They ride the horses through obstacle courses. Courses may include fences for the horses to jump over.

New Jersey officials did not pick one kind of horse to be the state animal. Each kind of horse has a different size, appearance, and color.

New Jerseyans own more than 600,000 horses.

More State Symbols

State Dinosaur: The hadrosaurus became the state dinosaur in 1991. In 1858, scientists found the first nearly whole dinosaur skeleton in Haddonfield. Scientists named it hadrosaurus after the town.

State Fish: Officials made the brook trout the state fish in 1991. Many brook trout live in New Jersey's rivers and streams.

State Folk Dance: The square dance became the state folk dance in 1983. This dance was popular among New Jersey's first settlers.

State Insect: New Jersey schoolchildren wanted the honeybee to be the state insect. The governor made their choice official in 1974. Honeybees carry pollen from plant to plant. Without pollen, New Jersey farmers would not be able to grow crops.

State Shell: Officials named the knobbed whelk the state shell in 1995. People often find knobbed whelks on New Jersey's beaches.

Speckled trout is another name for brook trout.

Places to Visit

Atlantic City Boardwalk

In 1870, Atlantic City built the first boardwalk in the world. This wooden sidewalk allows people to stay out of sand as they walk along the beach. Today, more than 30 million visitors walk along the boardwalk each year. They shop, eat, or walk on the beach. They also enjoy amusement rides.

Edison National Historic Site

The Edison National Historic Site is in West Orange. Thomas Edison's home and research laboratory stand on the site. Edison is one of the world's best-known inventors. The light bulb and movie camera are two of his many inventions. Visitors tour Edison's work space and 29-room house.

New Jersey State Aquarium

The New Jersey State Aquarium is in Camden. More than 4,000 fish and aquatic animals live in the aquarium. One of its tanks holds 760,000 gallons (2,876,904 liters) of water. Visitors tour more than 80 exhibits. At one exhibit, visitors may pet small sharks and stingrays.

Words to Know

cornucopia (kore-nuh-KOH-pee-uh)—a horn-shaped container for food; the cornucopia is a symbol for plenty.

equestrian (i-KWESS-tree-uhn)—having to do with horseback riding

laboratory (LAB-ruh-tor-ee)—a room or building with equipment for scientific experiments

mural (MYU-ruhl)—a large painting on a wall

prosperity (prahs-PAYR-uh-tee)—doing very well or being a success

rural (RUR-uhl)—having to do with the countryside or farming

Read More

Bock, Judy and Rachel Kranz. *Scholastic Encyclopedia of the United States.* New York: Scholastic, 1997.

Kummer, Patricia K. *New Jersey.* One Nation. Mankato, Minn.: Capstone Press, 1998.

Stein, R. Conrad. *New Jersey.* America the Beautiful. New York: Children's Press, 1998.

Welsbacher, Anne. *New Jersey.* United States. Minneapolis: Abdo & Daughters, 1998.

Useful Addresses

Division of Travel and Tourism
20 West State Street
P.O. Box 826
Trenton, NJ 08625-0826

New Jersey Secretary of State
State House
P.O. Box 300
Trenton, NJ 08625

Internet Sites

Kids Page—The State Seal and Symbols
http://www.njleg.state.nj.us/html98/njsymb.htm
New Jersey State Aquarium's Official Site
http://www.njaquarium.org
Stately Knowledge: NJ: Just the Facts
http://www.ipl.org/youth/stateknow/nj1.html
World's First Dinosaur Skeleton *Hadrosaurus Foulkii*
http://www.levins.com/dinosaur.html

Index